NORTH AMERICAN INDIAN CEREMONIES

NORTH AMERICAN
INDIAN
CEREMONIES
KAREN LIPTAK

FRANKLIN WATTS
NEW YORK/LONDON/TORONTO/SYDNEY
A FIRST BOOK

Library of Congress Catologing-in-Publication Data

Liptak, Karen.

    North American Indian ceremonies by Karen Liptak.
      p. cm.—(A First book)
    Includes bibliographical references and index.
    Summary: Describes a variety of Indian tribal ceremonies
and rituals, including those for war and peace, hunting and
gathering, and healing.
    ISBN 0-531-20100-7
    1. Indians of North America—Rites and ceremonies—
Juvenile literature.   2. Indians of North America—Social
life and customs—Juvenile literature. |1. Indians of North
America—Rites and ceremonies. 2. Indians of North
America—Social life and customs.| I. Title.
II. Series.
E98.R3L37   1992
299'.74—dc20   91-30263 CIP AC

The author extends her warm thanks to the following: Emory Sekaquaptewa, Hopi Nation; Kevin Locke and Winona Flying Earth, Hunkpapa Lakota (Sioux) Nation; Michael Darrow, Chiricahua Apache Historian; Leland Hemlock, Faithkeeper of the Longhouse for the Seneca Nation; and especially to Martha Kreipe de Montano.

Contents

A nineteenth-century pictograph
of a Sioux village shows the many
aspects of the Indians' daily lives.

A WAY OF LIFE

Today, as in the past, the lives of North American Indians are enriched by many ceremonies. These traditional events range from large, many-day tribal festivities to daily, private rituals. But each ceremony, big or small, helps the participants to strengthen their bonds with their heritage.

Many Native American ceremonies are a form of worship. In performing them, the people honor the Creator (often called the Great Spirit), Mother Earth, and human life. Also honored with ceremonies are plants and animal life and the various spirit forms of wind, fire, air, and water.

Ceremonies are held for many purposes. Some celebrate the milestones in life, such as birth and marriage. Others are annual holidays of thanksgiving. At initiation ceremonies, new members are brought into secret societies; at healing ceremonies, rituals are followed to prevent or cure illnesses. There are also ceremonies to prepare warriors (or today's soldiers) for battle and to welcome them home afterward. And, as in former times, some Native Americans continue to perform rituals every day; they will not pick a plant, hunt an animal, or eat a meal without the proper prayer.

Various objects used at one time in daily
Indian life, from weapons and utensils
to ceremonial objects

While ceremonies differ by region and by tribe, there are similar elements in many of them. Ceremonial costumes are often worn. Some include masks that are great works of art, like the wooden masterpieces carved by tribes on the Pacific Northwest Coast. Masks frequently represent the spirits of animals, plants, and spiritual beings and are said to give special power to the wearer.

In the old days, when buffalo were plentiful, ceremonial robes made from their hides were worn on the Great Plains. Ceremonial clothes woven from mountain goat wool and from the fur of special small dogs were highly valued on the Pacific Northwest Coast. Today, elegant outfits, some handed down for many generations, are still worn for special ceremonies.

Native American ceremonies often include rhythmic chanting and dancing, frequently accompanied by musical instruments. The most widely used instruments are drums and rattles, which are made from a variety of materials. Many drums are made from wood and animal skins. But canoes, logs, boxes, and baskets can all become drums, as long as you can bang on them!

Rattles might be made from hollow gourds (a kind of fruit), wood, animal skins, shells, or anything else that can be filled with noisemakers and shaken. Stones, seeds, sand, and corn are good noisemakers.

Left: This double-headed drum of the Plains
Indians was used both to cure the sick
and in ceremonial dancing.
Right: This Sioux rattle is made from
rawhide and buffalo and is
filled with pebbles.

In certain ceremonies sacred objects are required. One such item used throughout the continent is the sacred pipe, for which a special supply of tobacco is reserved. Puffing on the sacred pipe is said to bring the smoker closer to the Great Spirit, who is symbolically in the pipe's smoke. Non-Indians call the sacred pipe a "peace pipe" because smoking it with tribal members often came before the signing of a treaty.

Every pipe ceremony has a series of steps, from opening the bundle in which the pipe is stored to filling the pipe, smoking it, passing it around, and putting it away. Each part has its own strict rules, prayers, and rituals.

Tribal leaders often have several pipes, some for less important occasions and at least one that is used only for the group's major decisions. When a great decision has to be made, tribal members sit in a circle and pass the pipe around. Each person takes a few puffs and thinks about the decision at hand before passing the pipe to the next person.

Another important ceremonial object is the prayer stick, used today in many rituals by Indians of the American Southwest. These carved wooden sticks with feathers attached are believed able to attract the spirits. While saying the proper prayers, a person places the sticks at sacred shrines and around objects that require blessing.

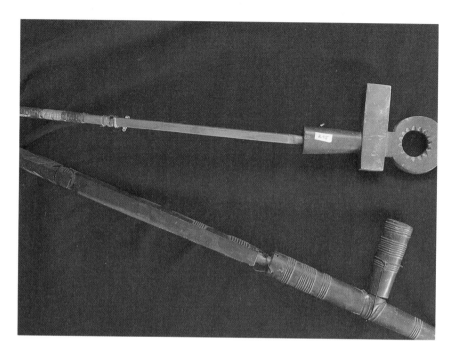

Nineteenth-century peace pipes

Most Native Americans purify themselves before a ceremony. This often calls for a food fast and a cleansing ritual, known as a sweat bath. A sweat bath can also be a ceremony on its own, with songs, prayers, offerings, and smoking of the sacred pipe. People sit in an enclosed structure called a sweat lodge while cold water is sprinkled over hot rocks inside the lodge. Steam forms, making the bathers sweat and cleansing them in body and mind.

Sweat lodges were used to prepare for many different kinds of ceremonies.

Some Cherokees of today still precede each tribal function with a traditional dip in the Long Man, their term for the river. Long Man is considered so powerful that polluting a river is strictly forbidden, lest Long Man respond to the insult with disease.

As in the past, taking part in tribal ceremonies and rituals helps North American Indian children learn about their culture, the world around them, and themselves. At the same time, these occasions help them grow closer to other tribal members.

THE LIFE CYCLE

Birth and Child Naming

Birth is a time of great joy, for a new life means that the tribe, as well as the family, will continue. In the old days, when a North American Indian woman was ready to give birth, she usually went to a separate structure or room. There, other women, including a midwife, cared for her and the newborn. Traditionally, the father did not see the baby until some days after birth. By then, many rituals had already taken place.

The Hopi Indians live in the American Southwest. Today, as in former times, a Hopi baby's grandmother on its father's side leads the preparations for the newborn child's "naming ceremony." (Many other tribes also have special naming ceremonies.) This is a very important event, held twenty days after birth. Until then, a Hopi baby has no name.

Before dawn on the naming day, the baby receives its name in a ceremony at which the father sees his new child for the first time. Then, as the sun rises, the mother and the father's mother present the baby to the sun and repeat the new name.

The Navajo Indians, the Hopi's neighbors, chant a special song at important times in a person's life. This song, called the Blessing Way, is performed to

These *amulets*, or charms, were containers
for a child's umbilical cord. They were worn
by young children and were later thrown away.

ensure health, harmony, and prosperity. The song tells
a story from the Navajo people's past and is first sung
for a baby as it is about to be born.

Later on in life, the Blessing Way song is chanted
at other special occasions and brings blessings for
everything—new homes (called hogans), tribal offi-
cers, livestock, ritual objects—and more. During the
Blessing Way, corn pollen, which is considered sacred,
is sprinkled on the person being blessed, as well as
on spectators, ceremonial objects, and the house where
the song is being sung.

Among the Cherokee, the number seven is sacred. Therefore, on a Cherokee baby's seventh day of life, traditionalists in the tribe still take him or her to Long Man. There the medicine person prays for the baby while holding the newborn over the water. The baby is offered to the water seven times but does not touch it until the mother wets her fingers and gently places them on the baby.

These special rituals show how some of the various Native Americans welcomed and continue to welcome their newborns into the world.

Coming of Age

Puberty, the time when youngsters begin to develop into adults and become physically able to have children—usually between ages twelve and fourteen—is often marked with ceremonies and rituals. These differ from tribe to tribe and also between the sexes.

In the past, many tribes would isolate a girl when she first began to menstruate. She would go to a separate hut, with only other women and girls for company. Later, throughout her childbearing years, she would return to the hut during each monthly period. This was because menstruating women were considered powerful enough to endanger the outcome of hunts and battles.

In some groups, the initial isolation for a young girl was followed by a huge celebration. Among the Sioux on the Great Plains, a female's puberty celebration is said to be one of seven sacred rites from the Great Spirit. It is still held to honor the strong role that women play in the family, which the Sioux consider the basic building block of human society.

As part of the ceremony, a huge feast is held for the girl, at which the medicine person sings a chant to White Buffalo Calf Woman, the powerful spiritual being who brings the Sioux blessings from the Great Spirit. Then the medicine person instructs the girl in her adult duties and places a sacred eagle feather in her hair as a symbol of her new role in the tribe. Later, all of the guests receive gifts.

The Apaches of the Southwest continue to hold one of the most famous girls' puberty ceremonies in the world. The Western Apache honor several girls at once at this four-day event. Called the Sunrise Ceremony, the ceremony includes chants and dances as well as feasting, entertainment, and gift giving.

During these events, an older woman instructs each girl. Meanwhile, a singer leads the ritual chanting and directs the building of the sacred tepee, symbolizing the universe. Masked dancers who bring the blessings of the Mountain Spirits, sacred to the Apaches, perform each night. And every girl being

Navajo women grind cornmeal in preparation
for a puberty ceremony.

honored wears a beautiful costume, a copy of the one worn by White Painted Woman, the mother of all Apache people. This symbolizes the idea that the girls have special powers at this time.

At one part of the ceremony, each girl walks on an animal skin along a path sprinkled with holy pollen. This is to assure that she will live a long and happy life.

After the public festivities, the girls have four days of private rituals with their female attendants in an isolated hut. When they return home, they are considered women, ready for marriage.

In past centuries, many tribes marked a boy's puberty with a ritual known as a vision quest. Today, as Native Americans gain new pride in their heritage, this ritual is being revived.

In a vision quest, a boy goes off alone to seek a Guardian Spirit to protect and guide him throughout his life. The spirit gives the boy skills. In the past, these skills were often those that his father or a close male relative had. Some boys also receive special gifts, such as the power to heal. Among tribes of the Eastern Woodland and Plateau, boys as young as five years old were sometimes encouraged to seek a Guardian Spirit.

Unlike a girl's one-time puberty ritual, vision quests can be repeated many times during a man's life to help him renew his link with his Guardian Spirit.

Vision quest rituals are different in various tribes, but a boy usually prepares for one with a purifying bath in a sweat lodge or a river. He may also be instructed by a medicine person or a close male relative. Then he leaves his people behind and goes off to live alone in a simple shelter. There, without food or drink, he awaits a vision, which often comes in the form of an animal.

If the boy feels a need to break his fast before a vision appears, he returns home early and has to wait until the next year to try again. But if the boy returns with a vision, his family or a medicine person interprets the vision.

In many tribes, children receive a name at birth or shortly afterward. A girl generally keeps this name, but a boy exchanges his as he gets older for one that better describes his traits or achievements. A vision quest can help determine what a boy's grown-up tribal name should be. If his name is changed, another ceremony is often needed.

In the past, both boys and girls went on vision quests on the Plateau. In other areas, seeking a Guardian Spirit was generally limited to boys.

Courtship and Marriage

In the old days, courtship and marriage customs varied greatly among North American Indians. Some groups observed so few customs that two people became husband and wife simply by deciding to live together. Other groups had complex courtship rituals and lavish marriage ceremonies.

A Hopi marriage could take months of preparation. Traditional Hopis still observe the rituals that begin with the future bride going to the groom's house. During her first three days there, the girl shows her future mother-in-law how well she does household chores, such as grinding corn and preparing meals. Her temperament is also observed. On the fourth day, the bride and groom wash and twist their hair together to symbolize the mingling of their lives. Then they say their marriage vows with their mothers by their sides.

But the girl cannot leave her mother-in-law's house yet. First, the groom's male relatives (with help from other men in the community) must weave a cotton marriage gown for her. They also must make a reed holder to carry it. While the men work, the new bride cooks meals for everyone busy on her behalf.

When her wedding dress is ready, the bride puts it on and walks alone to her mother's house. Later, the groom's family brings gifts to the bride's house. In return, her relatives prepare a special basket for the groom's family.

On the Pacific Northwest Coast, the parents of young Indian men and women in tribes such as the Tlingit had their spouses chosen for them by their

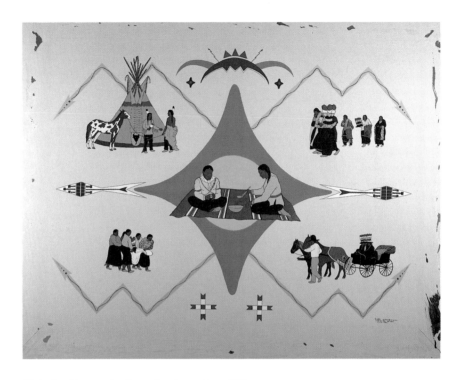

This Indian painting depicts the different parts of a marriage ceremony.

parents. Marriage was a way to strengthen a family's social position and wealth, both of which were very important to Native Americans in this region.

A courtship began with the boy's family offering the girl's family as many valuable gifts as it could afford. The offering showed how much the family thought the girl was worth. If the gifts were accepted, marriage plans could begin. Then the girl's family gave

A Hopi painting portrays the wedding payment.

gifts to the groom's family, making sure that they were as generous as possible.

Groups with this ritual usually expected families to continue exchanging gifts at major ceremonies throughout the couple's married life. Today young men and women have much more voice in choosing marriage partners than before. However, some families still keep the gift-exchange ritual.

As in former times, marriage among the Pacific Northwest Coast Indians is marked by the major ceremony of the potlatch. This is an important social affair that includes a gift-giving ritual and a huge feast, as well as music, song, and dance theater. Potlatches used to last for several days and were also held on many other occasions, to celebrate births, puberty, battle victories, the building of new homes, and the erection of totem poles. The largest potlatches marked one leader's death and the rise of a new leader to replace the old one.

In the past, the main purpose of the potlatch was to prove a host's rank and wealth. This was shown by all the host provided the guests in gifts, food, and performances.

Much socializing went on at potlatches. Guests caught up on the latest news, played games, and feasted on great amounts of food, which typically included smoked salmon, venison, berries, and roots. The potlatch was also the time when youngsters were initiated into secret societies and babies were named.

But no potlatch was over until the host gave out gifts to the guests. In return, the host would get many gifts when the guests held potlatches. The gifts were carefully distributed according to each guest's worth; the richest person received the most costly gifts. If a

A contemporary ceremony called
the Honor Giveaway is like the
potlatch in some ways.

man thought his gift was below his rank, his whole family felt insulted, and that could result in the host getting a meager gift at a future potlatch. Potlatches in modified form are still observed up and down the Pacific Northwest Coast.

Initiation into Secret Societies

Many North American Indian groups have secret societies. Some are open to all tribal members when they come of age. Others have rules that allow in new members by sex, heredity, or special traits, such as healing power or bravery in battle. The new members must pass through initiation rites to become part of the secret society.

One secret society in the American Southwest is the Kachina Society. The kachinas are spirit beings that the Hopi, Zuni, and other Pueblo groups call upon to bring rain and general harmony. The people say that the kachinas once lived among them. Then, after a big argument, the kachinas left, refusing to return. However, they agreed to let the people represent them in Pueblo ceremonies held during six months of the year. Hopi boys and girls who enter the Kachina Society learn the secrets of the kachinas at their initiation ceremony.

The ceremony, held in February, begins when the children of the community gather in the kiva, an un-

Zuni kachina dolls made of wood, cloth, and feathers

derground ceremonial shelter. There, while each child's ceremonial sponsor (usually a girl's mother and a boy's father) stands nearby, stories from the Hopi past are told by the Kachina Father. He is a respected member of the community. When he is finished, he sprinkles the children with cornmeal and blesses them.

Afterward, an eerie howling is heard from above, and three scary-looking kachinas climb down the ladder leading into the kiva. These are the Mother Kachina and her two whippers. As each child watches in fear and amazement, unexpected, yet traditional events take

A kachina dance on a Hopi
reservation in Arizona

place. When these are over, the Kachina Father pre-
sents cornmeal and sacred feathers to the boys and
girls before they leave the kiva.

At a ritual held the next dawn, each child receives
a ceremonial name. Days later, the children who are
entering the Kachina Society are told secrets about
the kachinas. They are sworn to silence so that younger
children will not learn the secrets or know what will
happen at their own initiation.

On the Pacific Northwest Coast, the Kwakiutl Indians have secret dancing societies into which their

young people are initiated during the Winter Ceremony of Tsitsika (which means "time when nothing is real"). The most elite of these societies is the Hamatsa, or Cannibal Dancers.

The Hamatsa annual initiation ceremony is meant to impress nonmembers with the society's power. Early in the morning on the ceremony day, established Hamatsa members blow on their secret whistles. This is the signal for other members to "kidnap" the young men and women initiates. In the drama that is then played out, the new members are symbolically taken to the home of a spirit known as the Cannibal-at-the-North-End-of-the-World. Actually, they are escorted to the woods or to the back of a house, where they are taught the rituals and dances of the Hamatsa.

When they return, in ceremonial clothes, they act as if they are under the Cannibal's power and wildly bite people on their arms. Members of another secret society, the Bear-men, then appear and wreck people's property. But nobody panics; records are kept of all of the damage so that everything can be replaced.

Society members then calm down the initiates in private and public ceremonies that often involve magic. The public events are held in the village's ceremonial house, where Cannibal Dancers in elaborately painted masks enact the stories of their ancestors. These ceremonies have two purposes. They show audiences how the powerful society can calm the spirit, and they also reveal that the initiates are now in control of the spirit.

Death

Death, always a mystery, is acknowledged by Native Americans in a variety of ways. Some groups, like the Hopi, have relatively simple ceremonies when someone dies.

Today; as in the past, Hopis cover the face of a deceased tribal member with a cotton mask, symbolic of the rain cloud. A Hopi woman is buried in her marriage gown, and a Hopi man is dressed in clothing to represent his station in life. The body is carried to a secluded place where mourners silently lower it into a grave, around which they place prayer sticks. Then the grave is covered, and a bowl of food is left nearby to symbolically feed the soul on its journey to the spirit world.

Four days later, the women mourners return to the gravesite and place another bowl of food there. After that, the soul is believed to have safely traveled to the spirit world, and the women go back to their normal routine.

In other tribes, a death calls for enormous ceremonies. The Indians of the Iroquois Confederation in the Northeast believe that a dead person's spirit will

The title of this painting by Seth Eastman
is "Feeding the Dead" and describes what
was part of a death ceremony.

not depart until the Tenth Day Feast. On this occasion,
ten days after someone dies, all his or her possessions
are given away, and the person's favorite foods are
served. A year of mourning follows, ending with a second feast on the anniversary of the death.

Other Iroquoian groups, such as the Seneca, continue to hold an annual all-night ceremony at which
all of the dead of the community are honored.

WAR AND PEACE CEREMONIES AND RITUALS

Many North American Indian groups hold war dances and other ceremonies to prepare warriors for a coming battle. Such events still take place. In 1991, Apaches at the San Carlos Reservation in Arizona held a four-day ceremony, led by a medicine person, before eight men from the reservation left with the United States armed forces to fight in the Persian Gulf War.

In the past, before Plains Indians went to war, they set up a ceremonial camp outside their home village. There they sang war songs and observed food restrictions and other taboos to prepare for the up-coming battle. Later, after entering enemy territory, they held additional rituals to bring their spirit helpers to guide and protect them on the battlefield.

Plains Indians, such as the Sioux, also performed a ritual during battle: that of using a coup stick to strike an enemy. A coup stick is a thin wooden lance with feathers attached. Warriors were not considered brave unless they got close enough to an enemy for a strike, although killing was not necessary.

Among many tribes, bravery in battle earned one the right to receive a new name, often chosen by the leader of the war party. A new title also might be bestowed on an outstanding warrior.

A Sioux coup stick was used by warriors to strike the enemy. Coup sticks were also carried as symbols of authority, and thus served both a ceremonial and a practical function.

When warriors came home from fighting, ceremonies were frequently performed to celebrate their return and to cleanse them. Young Natchez warriors of the Southeast were respectfully escorted by musicians and other warriors to a special place. Here their faces were smeared with war medicine as part of the ceremony honoring them.

A warbonneted elder

The next day, purification rituals took place, followed by a round of festivities that lasted for three days and included many feasts, dancing, and very little sleep.

When some groups in the Northeast and Great Lakes region were victorious, the warriors were honored in ceremonies at the community lodge. There the warriors were encouraged to dance, while chanting in great detail about their war feats. However, lying about battle victories was strictly discouraged.

HUNTING AND GATHERING RITUALS

Before hunting parties set out, almost every Indian tribe performs rituals that include prayers to the animals so that they will allow the people to hunt them. Many North American Indian groups also perform rituals before they plant or gather fruits, vegetables, and other crops, such as cotton and tobacco.

On the Pacific Northwest Coast, salmon was the main food of many tribes for centuries. Even today, certain tribes in this region, such as the Quinault and Tsimshian, hold annual ceremonies when the salmon return from the Pacific Ocean to the rivers in which

One of the many agricultural rituals was the corn dance, which is still performed today.

they were born. During these events, known as the Salmon Rites, the undamaged skeleton of the first salmon taken that year from a river is returned to its waters. Since Indians here believe in rebirth, these ceremonies are held to make sure that the salmon will be reborn without any bones missing.

Where the whale was hunted on the Pacific Northwest Coast, as among the Nootka, the whaling leader inherited his position. He was said to have great religious power. Before a hunt began, he retired to a special prayer structure, where he was surrounded by the skulls of previous whale leaders. There, in secret rituals, he asked his Guardian Spirit for a successful hunt. On the Plains, in the days when buffalo were plentiful, buffalo dances were sure to precede the departure of hunting expeditions.

Ceremonies are held after hunting as well as before. Each fall, the Tohono O'odham (formerly called the Papago) of the Southwest hold a Deer Dance. All the deer that have been hunted and plants that have been gathered are made safe for eating. The first deer of the season is cooked at this time, as the elder men of the community sing. Meanwhile, the young men and women, painted to look like ears of corn, dance in front of the deer meat and other food. But nobody can start eating until prayers are said.

Hopi Indians dance the Rainbow Dance at
Mesa Verde National Park, in southwestern
Colorado, for the first time in 500 years.

FERTILITY CYCLE

Throughout the year, North American Indians hold major ceremonies to give thanks for their blessings and to ask for abundant food and other good fortune in the future. One such annual holiday, celebrated by many tribes in the Southeast and Northeast, is the Busk, or the Green Corn Ceremony.

The exact events of the Busk vary from group to group, but it is usually observed in the summer. Some groups hold Busk when the first corn is ready; others, when the last crop ripens.

In the past, the first day of Busk was spent cleaning up; the women cleaned their homes while the men repaired the community council lodge. Then the sacred fire in the lodge and the cooking fires in each home were put out.

The people fasted on the second day and feasted on the third. Then came the fourth and most important day of Busk. After the men bathed in the river at dawn, the medicine person put four ears of new corn on the fire logs in the council house and relit the sacred fire. Following this, some of the village's most honored men and women danced the Green Corn Dance around the flames. The Green Corn Dance is itself a prayer, asking the Great Spirit to protect the people. Afterward, other villagers joined in the rites and officially welcomed the new year.

Women rekindled their home fires with coals from the sacred fire. Then they cooked a great feast, which the men ate separately from the women and children. After the meal, they all gathered together to hear the village leader's speech. Later, everyone was purified for the new year by bathing in a nearby body of water.

Today, in the American Northeast, groups like the Seneca observe the Green Corn Dance as one of many ceremonies on their yearly calendar. These begin with the Maple Dance in the early spring. Leland Hemlock, a Faith Keeper in the Longhouse for the Seneca, explains that this ceremony takes place when "Mother Earth is waking up and the sap starts flowing."

The Seneca and other northeastern Native Americans also perform the Seed Ceremony, Sun Ceremony, and Thunder Ceremony. A Strawberry Ceremony is held when the first fruits of the season come up; a Harvest Ceremony is held in October; and a Mid-Winter Ceremony, also known as the New Year's Ceremony, ends the yearly cycle.

Like the Green Corn Ceremony, all of these annual rites are family events at which the people thank the Creator for furnishing everything that's on the earth. By attending these events, "the children learn our language and our culture," says Mr. Hemlock.

On the Great Plains, the major annual ceremony

is the Sun Dance, held to offer thanksgiving to the Creator and to renew the spirit. It is also conducted to ask for healings or forgiveness for individuals or a group.

Sun Dances differ widely among tribes. The Sioux, who consider it one of seven rites from the Great Spirit to help them live a balanced life, used to hold a Sun Dance each summer. Sioux bands from miles around attended the twelve-day ceremony.

In former times, the ceremony began with four days of festivities, during which the medicine people chose assistants for the rites. This was also when vol-

This colorful painting by Archie Blackowl illustrates the Cheyenne Sun Dance.

unteers pledged to take part in the dance so that their prayers or those of the group would be heard.

Through the next four days, the medicine people taught the volunteers what the ceremony meant and how to perform it.

The last four days of the Sun Dance were the most sacred. On the first of them, a man set out to find the sacred cottonwood tree. He marked it with red paint. When he came back and announced his success, the Buffalo Dance was performed.

On the second sacred day, specially honored women left the camp to cut down the cottonwood. They performed rituals along the way and at the tree. Then they chopped down the cottonwood, stripped its bark, and carried the pole back to the campsite.

The next day, the cottonwood pole was painted, and sacred objects were placed on it. Then the pole was raised in the center of the roofless Sun Dance Lodge, and the warriors danced around it.

On the last sacred day, the dancers were painted. The Sioux Sun Dance involves sacrifice, and each dancer's colors and symbols signified how much pain he or she had volunteered to endure so that their request to the Great Spirit would be granted. Then the Buffalo Dance was performed once more, followed by a ceremonial piercing of the children's ears.

Now the great sacrifice began. Some of the dancers who had pledged to do so fasted and danced around

A Sun Dance lodge in Montana
is lit up by a sunset.

the pole until they fainted. Others cut bits of flesh from their bodies as offerings to the Great Spirit. Winona Flying Earth of the Hunkpapa Sioux explains that the sacrifice is now done by lifting a small piece of skin with a needle and then cutting it. In this way, volunteers show that "the physical world is of no importance in accomplishing a prayer."

The Sun Dance Ritual

The most honored dancers are those who experience the greatest sacrifice of the Sun Dance. Only men may do this.

Two slits are cut into skin they pinch up on their chests. A thin wooden rod is inserted in through one slit and out the other. Then leather strips that are tied to the cottonwood pole are attached to the rod.

The men lean against their leather strips until their skin naturally comes free from the rod and they fall down. This may take hours. But in this way, by enduring pain in their bodies—the one thing they own—they honor the Creator who gives them all else.

Meanwhile, other dancers circle the pole, their faces upward, so that their prayers are carried to the Creator on the rays of the sun. Throughout the ceremony, drummers play and singers chant sacred songs.

Although this seems like an ordeal, those who take part in the Sun Dance today say that the experience links them with the Great Spirit. At the same time, their willingness to suffer, often for the whole group, earns them great honor from their people. Instead of a twelve-day ceremony, the Sioux now hold smaller Sun Dances throughout the year, often when a family is having trouble or someone is ill.

In southwestern Pueblo villages, many annual ceremonies are held to honor the kachinas. Each year, at the time of the winter solstice, the kachinas journey from their home in the San Francisco Mountains to the Pueblos. The event is marked with a ceremony at which children receive gifts, including dolls and bows and arrows.

After spending six months among the people and helping them spiritually prepare for healthy crops, the kachinas pay their last visit of the year to the Pueblos. For the Hopi, this happens during the yearly Niman Dance in July. When it is nearly time for the summer solstice, Hopi men begin spending their nights in the kiva, preparing for this dance by praying, practicing their songs, and making prayer sticks and other ceremonial objects.

At the ceremony itself, the Kachina Father speaks to the kachinas on behalf of the whole community and symbolically feeds them sacred cornmeal. During Niman Day, the kachinas perform special dances many

The entrance to a kiva still in use today

times. But the year's brides are kept from seeing the kachinas until the end of the day. Then, wearing their wedding gowns, they are allowed to attend the very last dance.

The Niman Ceremony gives the kachinas another chance to distribute gifts, which include fruit and the first ears of corn. As the sun begins to set, the Kachina Father makes a plea on behalf of the people, asking that the kachinas remember them and come back as rain.

HEALING

Traditional Native American healing ceremonies involve many rituals. In the old days, sickness was often thought to come from a foreign object in the body, and even today, many healing rituals include the "sucking cure." This calls for the medicine person to use a tube of some kind, (usually made out of bone or wood) to "suck out" the irritating object from the patient's body.

Today, although American Indians use modern medicine, native healing rituals often are still performed for their spiritual benefits. Healing ceremonies may call for herbs, potions, and sacred objects, as well as rattles and whistles.

"Making Sweet Grass Medicine," a painting
by Joseph Henry Sharp, shows one of the rituals
followed in making a healing medicine.

Among the Iroquoian groups, members of the
False Face Society, wearing extravagantly carved masks,
perform in healing ceremonies. Each patient cured by
the society becomes a new member and can take part
in future False Face healing ceremonies.

In the Great Lakes region, the medicine society is
known as the Midewiwin, and its most dramatic rite

This painting by
Beatiean Yazz illustrates
one of the many
aspects of a Navajo
healing rite.

A member of a contemporary
False Face Society

is the Great Medicine Dance, at which new members are initiated. During this event, members thrust a sacred medicine bag filled with special shells toward the initiates. When the shells are directed at them, initiates fall down, as if in a trance. Later, they act as if filled with new power, which they show by rising and aiming their own medicine bags of shells at the other members.

The Navajo have perhaps the best-known Native American healing ceremonies. These events include chants that last up to nine days and are usually accompanied by dry paintings, known as sand paintings. Sand paintings are used in healing ceremonies by Tohono O'odham, Apache, and Pueblo medicine people, too. Most sand paintings are made on the ground with colored sandstone and are symbolic pictures from ancient stories. Food fasts, baths, sacred objects, holy pollen, and medicines are other elements in the healing ceremonies of many Southwestern Indians.

Among various Apache groups, curing an illness sometimes calls for a ritual in which four people perform traditional dances while circling the patient. The dancers, in masks, headdresses, and body paint, recreate a ceremony that the Apaches received from the Mountain Spirit people. These spiritual beings once lived among the Apaches and taught some of them useful ceremonies. During the dance performance, a

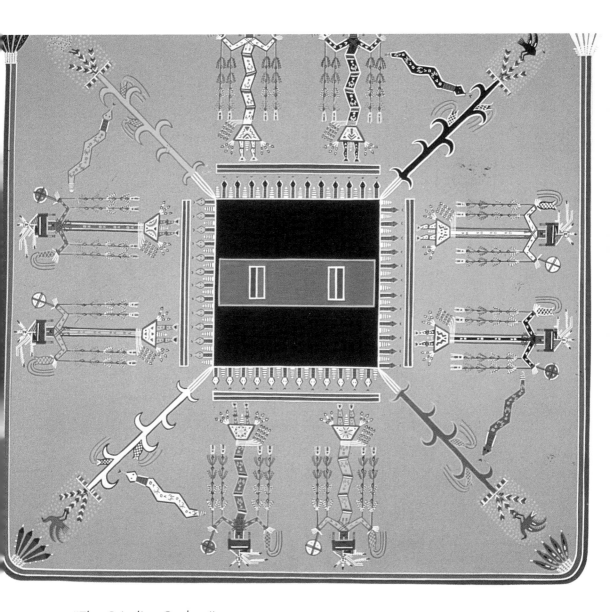

"The Grinding Snakes,"
a Navajo sand painting

medicine person, or someone else with authority, leads the Mountain Spirit Ceremony with the proper songs and prayers.

CEREMONIES OF TODAY

There are a great variety of North American Indian ceremonies, many of which are still performed. Today the ceremonies usually take place on reservations, and tribal members who live far away return home to share in them. Other events are held by Indians in cities and at Native American cultural centers, where watching and performing in them helps Indians feel pride in their history and heritage.

Some ceremonies on reservations are open to the public. Elsewhere, demonstrations of ceremonial dances are staged at Native American powwows, pageants, fairs, and museums throughout the country. These exhibitions give non-Indians a chance to see events that are normally closed to the public.

As in the past, some ceremonies and rituals continue to be held in secret. Sometimes, close non-Indian friends of tribal members are invited to these private, sacred affairs. However, Indian groups have secret societies that remain closed even to many tribal members as well as to outsiders.

The opening parade in the Red Earth Festival,
a contemporary Indian ceremony

If you want to attend a tribal ceremony, ask your state or local tourist bureau for a calendar of regional Native American events. Check with tourist bureaus in any areas you visit, as well. You can also find this information in books, perhaps at your public library. One useful book is *North American Indian Travel Guide* by Ralph and Lisa Shanks (Costano Books, Petaluma, CA 94953).

If you are privileged to attend a Native American ceremony, remember to be respectful of your hosts. Visitors should always check to be sure that they do not disregard any tribal rules. (For instance, taking pictures of some ceremonies is forbidden.) As a welcome guest, you will be able to share in the spectacle and the sacredness of a very special way of life.

GLOSSARY

Apache—North American Indians of the Southwest.

Cherokee—North American tribe, originally from the southeastern United States.

False Face Society—Healing group of the Iroquois Confederacy.

Hamatsa (Cannibal Dancers)—The most elite dancing society of the Kwakiutl Indians.

Hogan—An earth-covered home used by the Navajo.

Hopi—North American Indian tribe of the Southwest.

Iroquois—North American Indian Confederacy in central and western New York, today composed of six tribes (Cayugas, Mohawks, Onondagas, Oneidas, Senecas, and Tusaroras).

Kachina—Spirits that bring life-giving rain, as well as health, to the Pueblo Indian communities.

Kiva—A ceremonial shelter, usually below ground level, used by Pueblo Indians.

Kwakiutl—North American Indians of the Pacific Northwest Coast.

Long Man—Cherokee term for river.

Menstruation—The process of discharging blood and dead cell debris by adult women at approximately monthly intervals, beginning at puberty.

Midewiwin—The Great Medicine Society, in the Great Lakes region.

Midwife—A woman who assists other women in childbirth.

Niman ceremony—Last appearance each year of the kachinas in the Hopi community.

Natchez—North American Indian tribe of the Southeast.

Navajo—North American Indian tribe of the Southwest, today the largest Indian nation in the United States.

Nootka—North American Indian tribe of the Pacific Northwest.

Potlatch—Huge ceremonial feast at which gifts are given to guests.

Puberty—The stage of maturation in which a person becomes capable of sexual reproduction.

Pueblo—Village dwellings built of stone or adobe by certain southwestern tribes collectively called the Pueblo Indians.

Quinault—Pacific Northwest Coast Indians.

Seneca—Indian tribe of the Northeast, part of the Iroquois Confederacy.

Sioux—North American tribe of the Great Plains.

Sweat lodge—Enclosed structure in which cleansing rituals take place.

Tlingit—North American tribe living on the Pacific Northwest Coast.

Tohono O'odham (Papago)—North American tribe of the Southwest.

Totem pole—Wooden pole on which family crests, or totems, are represented.

Tsimshian—North American tribe of the Pacific Northwest Coast.

FOR FURTHER READING

Gobel, Paul. *Buffalo Woman*. Scarsdale, New York: Bradbury Press, 1984.

Liptak, Karen. *North American Indian Medicine People*. New York: Franklin Watts, 1990.

Marquis, Arnold. *A Guide To America's Indians: Ceremonials Reservations and Museums*. Norman, Oklahoma, and London: University of Oklahoma Press, 1974.

Mayhar, Ardath. *Medicine Walk*. New York: Atheneum, 1985 (fiction).

Mike, Jan. *Kachi A Hopi Girl: Historical Paper Doll Book to Read, Color and Cut*. Tucson: Treasure Chest Publications, 1989.

Ohiyesa (Charles A. Eastman). *Indian Boyhood*. Glorieta, New Mexico: Rio Grande Press, 1976.

Showers, Paul. *Indian Festivals*. New York: Crowell, 1969.

Wolfson, Evelyn. *Growing Up Indian*. New York: Walker, 1986.

INDEX

ABOUT THE AUTHOR

Karen Liptak has written many books on a variety of subjects, including Native Americans and the natural sciences. For Franklin Watts she has authored the five books in the North American Indian series, as well as *Saving Our Wetlands and Their Wildlife*. She lives in Tucson, Arizona, with her daughter, Jana.